Grasses

June Loves

CHELSEA CLUBHOUSE

An Imprint of Chelsea House Publishers
A Haights Cross Communications Company
Philadelphia

This edition first published in 2005 in the United States of America by Chelsea House Publishers, a subsidiary of Haights Cross Communications.

Chelsea House Publishers
2080 Cabot Boulevard West, Suite 201
Langhorne, PA 19047-1813

The Chelsea House world wide web address is www.chelseahouse.com

First published in 2005 by
MACMILLAN EDUCATION AUSTRALIA PTY LTD
627 Chapel Street, South Yarra, Australia 3141

Visit our website at www.macmillan.com.au

Associated companies and representatives throughout the world.

Copyright © June Loves 2005

Library of Congress Cataloging-in-Publication Data
Loves, June.
    Grass / June Loves.
    p. cm. – (Plants)
    Includes index.
    ISBN 0-7910-8269-5
    1. Grasses – Juvenile literature. I. Title.
    QK495.G74L67 2004
    584'.9–dc22

                                                    2004016336

Edited by Anna Fern
Text and cover design by Christine Deering
Page layout by Christine Deering
Photo research by Legend Images
Illustrations by Melissa Webb

Printed in China

Acknowledgements

The author and the publisher are grateful to the following for permission to reproduce copyright material:

Cover photograph: Sugar cane, courtesy of Ian D. Goodwin/AUSCAPE.

Jean-Paul Ferrero/AUSCAPE, p. 13; Ian D. Goodwin/AUSCAPE, pp. 1, 10; Australian Picture Library, pp. 12, 21; Australian Picture Library/Corbis, p. 27; Corbis Digital Stock, pp. 7, 11, 17 (top and bottom); The DW Stock Picture Library, p. 22; Getty Images, pp. 3, 23, 26, 28; Getty Images/Photodisc, p. 20; Photodisc, pp. 4, 5, 6, 8, 9, 30; Steve Lovegrove/Picture Tasmania Photo Library, pp. 16, 29.

While every care has been taken to trace and acknowledge copyright, the publisher tenders their apologies for any accidental infringement where copyright has proved untraceable. Where the attempt has been unsuccessful, the publisher welcomes information that would redress the situation.

E584.9

Contents

Plants

Plants are living things. They grow all over the world, in hot and cold places.

Plants such as grasses provide food for many animals.

Grass

Grass is a flowering plant with long, hollow leaves. Grass plants growing closely together can make a soft, green lawn for playing and resting.

Hundreds of grass plants grow together to make a lawn.

Where Grass Grows

Grass grows in many different places. It can grow in swamps, **deserts**, **alpine regions**, and hot **tropical areas**.

Some grasses can survive in hot, dry deserts.

Many kinds of grass are very tough plants. They grow well in hot and cold **climates**. They can even survive in long periods of **drought**.

Some grasses can survive freezing temperatures.

Grasslands

A grassland is an area where grass is the main plant. Grasslands are important for animals. They provide homes and food for many animals, birds, and insects.

Natural grasslands are places where wild animals feed.

Farms

Many kinds of grass are grown on farms. Grass is grown to feed grazing animals such as cattle, sheep, horses, and goats. Crops of grass plants such as rice and wheat are grown to feed people.

Grass is grown on this farm to feed sheep.

Kinds of Grass

There are many different kinds of grass.

Sugarcane

Sugarcane is a kind of grass. The sweet juice of these tall plants is used to make sugar.

Sugarcane is grown in hot tropical places.

Cereals

Cereal grasses, such as wheat, rice, oats, barley, and corn are grown for their seeds, or grain. Cereals are the most important food for people in all parts of the world.

Wheat seeds are ground up into flour to make bread.

Pasture

Many kinds of grass are grown on farms to feed grazing animals. These grasses can be cut and dried to make hay and straw to feed to animals.

Farm animals are fed hay and straw when there is not enough fresh grass.

Bamboo

Bamboo is a kind of grass. Bamboo plants are tough and woody and can grow as tall as houses. Bamboos grow in Central and North America, Africa, and parts of Asia.

A panda's main food is the new leaves of bamboo plants.

Parts of Grass

Grass plants have long thin leaves and hollow stems. They have strong **roots**, and can send out **shoots** that spread along the ground.

flowers

stem

leaf

shoot

bud

roots

Grasses are flowering plants.

Grass flowers grow in groups, called spikelets.

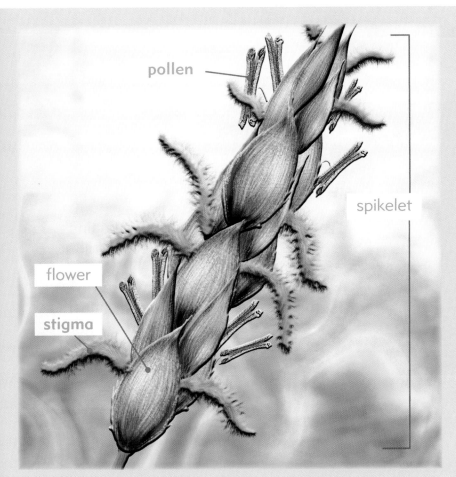

pollen

spikelet

flower

stigma

A spikelet is made up of many flowers.

How Grass Grows

Most grasses grow from seeds.
A seed contains a tiny plant
and a storage of food to
help the plant grow.

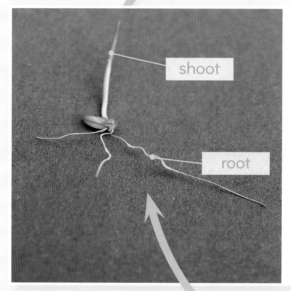

shoot

root

A seed remains
in the soil until it
is time to grow.
The seed grows a
root down into the
soil, and a shoot
up into the air.

The grass plant gets bigger until flowers grow at the top of the stalk. The flowers then produce seeds.

The seeds fall to the ground. Some grass plants live for one year, then die back after they make seeds. Other grass plants keep growing from year to year.

How Grass Makes Seeds

To make seeds, grass flowers need a special dust from the flowers of other grass plants, called pollen. When the grass flower is in full bloom, pollen is released into the air and is carried by the wind to other flowers.

flower

pollen

Grass flowers produce a lot of pollen, which is carried to other grass flowers by the wind.

Part of the flower called the stigma hangs outside the flower to catch pollen floating in the wind. This is called **pollination**. When the grass flower has been pollinated, it grows seeds.

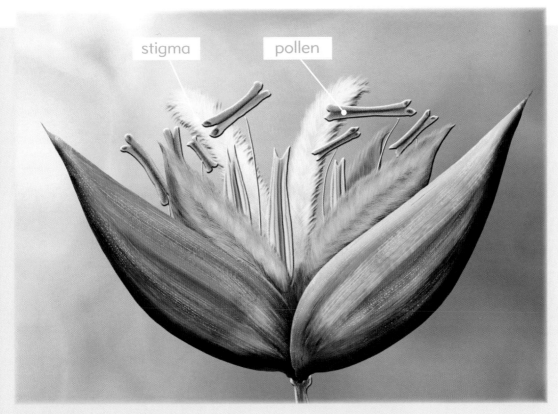

A stigma that hangs out like this has a good chance of catching some pollen as it flies by.

New Shoots

New shoots grow from the bottom of the stem of a grass plant. If the upper part of the grass blade is cut, new shoots continue to grow from buds close to the ground. Grasses can also regrow by putting out shoots along the ground.

Grass keeps growing after animals graze on it.

Helpers for Growing Grass

Grazing animals and fires can help new grass plants to grow strong and healthy. Grazing animals return **nutrients** to the soil in their droppings. Grass fires remove dead plant material and weeds, and add nutrients to the soil.

Fires can help grass to grow.

Growing Grass

You can grow a soft green lawn to rest on, or you can grow more decorative grass plants. Like most plants, grasses need soil, water, and light to grow well.

Grass can be grown to be very decorative.

Some grasses, such as wild grasses, do not need heavy watering. Others need a lot of water to grow well.

Some wild grasses are popular garden plants.

Grow a Hairy Henry

Watch Hairy Henry's hair grow!

What you need:

- old nylon tights
- a handful of grass seeds
- one or two cups of soil
- two elastic bands
- buttons and beads for decoration
- glue
- shallow dish
- water

What to do:

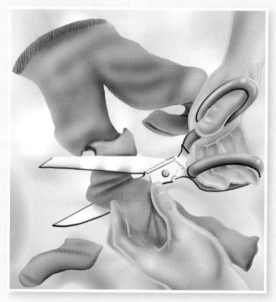

1 Cut a 12-inch (30-centimeter) strip from the nylon tights.

2 Tie a knot in one end and turn it inside out so that you have a bag.

3 Put the grass seeds inside the bag and fill it with soil. Tie the end of the bag with a knot or elastic band.

4 Pinch out a nose and tie it with an elastic band. Glue on buttons and beads for eyes and a mouth.

5 Soak Hairy Henry in water and place him in the dish. Keep the dish topped up with water and wait for Henry's hair to sprout.

Tips for Gardeners

Grass plants are easy to grow.

- Be careful not to mow your lawn too short. This can damage the grass roots and new shoots.

Planting bamboo in a pot will stop it from spreading where it is not wanted.

- Use lawn clippings as **mulch** on other parts of the garden.

- Always wash your hands when you have finished gardening.

Mowing the lawn encourages new shoots to grow at the base of the grass plants.

Useful Grass

Grass has many uses. People all over the world depend on grass cereal crops for food. Some grasses can be woven into fabric. Grasses can even be used to make **thatched** roofs.

This house has a thatched roof.

Bamboo is a very light, but strong grass. It is used to make houses, bridges, and furniture.

Bamboo is strong enough to be used as scaffolding for work to be done on this building.

Amazing Grass

There are about 10,000 different kinds of grass. Grass roots form a tough mat that helps stop the soil from being washed or blown away. Grass can regrow from old roots, and can survive droughts, fires, and being eaten by animals.

YOU CAN HELP SAVE THE BEACH
PLEASE USE WALKOVERS
FOOT TRAFFIC WILL KILL VEGETATION

Grasses help hold these sand dunes together.

Glossary

alpine region   high mountain area

bud   top of a shoot or branch where new leaves or flowers grow

climate   the usual weather in a place

desert   a very dry place with few plants

drought   a time without rain

mulch   a layer of chopped-up leaves or other plant material to help stop the soil from drying out and stop weeds from growing

nutrients   food in the soil that a plant can use to grow

pollen   fine yellow dust made in the center of a flower

pollination   movement of pollen from one flower to another

root   part of a plant that grows down into the soil and takes in water and nutrients

shoot   young branch or stem of a plant

stigma   the sticky ending of the female part of a flower, which catches pollen from other flowers during pollination

thatched   grasses bunched and tied together to make a structure, such as a roof

tropical area   a place where the weather is warm and wet

Index